Dedicated to my two boys. I will always be proud of you.

Stay in touch at www.piccopuppy.com and @PiccoPuppy on Instagram and Facebook.

Picco Puppy books are available in personalized, bilingual, French, Spanish, Italian, German, Chinese, and Japanese editions. Visit www.piccopuppy.com for more information.

A special thanks to my wonderful team: Zina Iugai (illustrator) and Brooke Vitale (editor).

Font Credits
Lost Brush by Stripes Studio
Marck Script by Denis Masharov
Cormorant Upright by Christian Thalmann
Century Schoolbook by Morris Fuller Benton
Copse by Dan Rhatigan
Josefin Sans by Santiago Orozco

Text and illustrations © 2022 Picco Puppy. All rights reserved. No part of this publication may be reproduced, stored in a retrieval system, or transmitted in any form or by any means, electronic, mechanical, photocopying, recording, or otherwise, without written permission of the publisher, except where permitted by law.

First published in 2022 by Picco Puppy
Marketing Munch Pty Ltd DBA Picco Puppy, PO Box 103 Killara NSW 2071 Australia
Picco Puppy is a registered trademark of Marketing Munch Pty Limited

A catalogue record for this book is available from the National Library of Australia
ISBN 978-1-922638-03-8

I Will Always Be Proud of You

MICHAEL WONG • ZINA IUGAI

I look at you, my little one,
and feel a sense of pride.

The love that grows inside my heart
is one I cannot hide.

One day, I know you'll spread your wings,
and then you will fly free.

Today I watch you, wondering
what you'll grow up to be.

Will you enrich our souls with wondrous music or wise words?

Or cook the most delightful meals
that help to warm the heart.

Will you rush into danger so
that you can save the day,

Or nurse the sick to health again
so that they all may play?

It may be that you'll someday care
for those in need of aid,

Or coach all kinds of athletes so they'll reach their highest grade.

Perhaps you will empower kids
to be all they can be,

Or maybe you'll find ways to save the creatures of the sea.

Will you one day discover how
to cure the common cold?

Or maybe you'll show kindness that
is valued more than gold.

It might be that you'll turn our waste
to something that has worth,

Or pioneer clean energy
to make a healthy Earth.

Will you turn your thoughts skyward to what's waiting in the stars?

Or will you build a wonderful
new world for us on Mars?

Your passion waits, so seek it out
to find the truest you,

And strive to be the best you can
in everything you do.

When clouds of doubt turn sunshine to a dark and hazy gray,

Stay strong and know tomorrow always brings a brighter day.

I have no doubt you'll reach your dreams
and get there without fear.

Just know that if you ever need me,
I will be right here.

I wish you happiness, no matter what you choose to do.

I love you and . . .

I always will be very proud of you!

Can You Spot the Famous People?

No matter what obstacles you face, believe in yourself and all that you are—
just like these famous people did. Can you spot all five in the book?

Can you spot a young Annie Jump Cannon?
Annie Jump Cannon was born in 1863. She was a pioneer in the field of astronomy. Cannon classified about 350,000 stars by their spectral characteristics (temperature, color, size, brightness, and composition).

Can you spot a young Bessie Coleman?
Bessie Coleman was born in 1892. In 1921, she became the first African-American woman and Native American to earn a pilot's license. She was known as "Brave Bessie" for doing dangerous stunts at air shows.

Can you spot a young Friedrich Fröbel?
Friedrich Fröbel was born in 1782. At the time, children under the age of seven did not attend school. Fröbel's belief that young children should be educated changed that. In 1837, he opened the first "kindergarten."

Can you spot a young Ludwig van Beethoven?
Ludwig van Beethoven was born in 1770. He is one of the greatest composers of all time. Amazingly enough, Beethoven wrote some of his greatest works after going deaf. His music is still popular today.

Can you spot a young Vincent van Gogh?
Vincent van Gogh was born in 1853. He is a famous painter, known best for Starry Night and Sunflowers. Van Gogh did not start painting until he was 27. He painted about 900 paintings in ten years.

Can You Spot the Dogs?

There are 22 dogs in the book. Can you spot them all?

 Bernese Mountain Dog
 Bichon Frise
 Border Collie
 Brussels Griffon
 Bulldog
 Cairn Terrier

 Cane Corso
 Chesapeake Bay Retriever
 Chihuahua
 Chow Chow
 Cocker Spaniel
 Collie

 Coton de Tulear
 Dachshund
 Labrador Retriever
 Miniature Schnauzer
 Old English Sheepdog
 Rottweiler

 Russell Terrier
 Samoyed
 Scottish Terrier
 Shih Tzu

Hi, it's Michael here. Did you know there are more books in "The Unconditional Love Series"? I hope you collect them all. Available at PiccoPuppy.com and all good bookstores.

Win a hardcover every month and claim your gift at www.piccopuppy.com/gift.

Michael Wong is an award-winning children's author. He is passionate about creating empowering, diverse, and inclusive books for kids. Michael lives with his wife and two children in Sydney, Australia.

Zina Jugai is an artist who fills her illustrations with light and atmosphere. She dreams of creating magical worlds with her illustrations.

The Unconditional Love Series

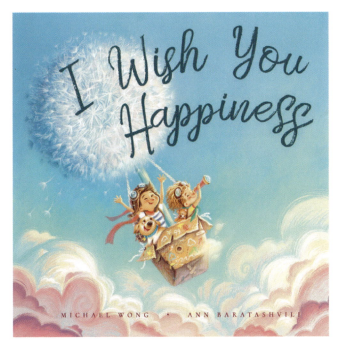

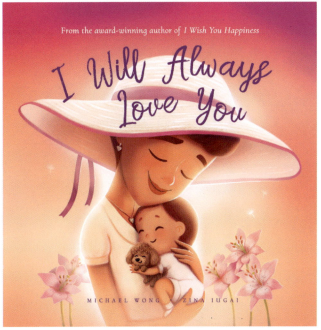

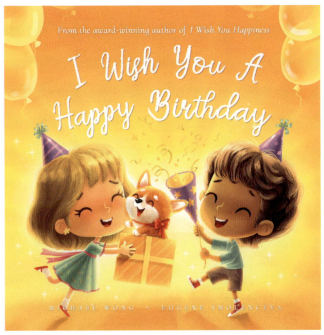

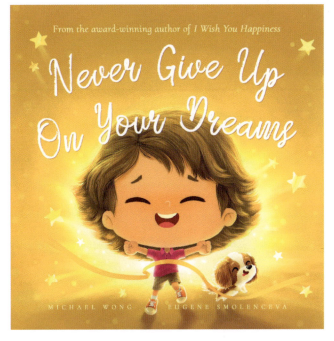

Printed in Poland
by Amazon Fulfillment
Poland Sp. z o.o., Wrocław